MW01628451

FOREWORD BY
NANCY GUTHRIE

THE CHRISTMAS STORY

Tracing Glory

THROUGH THE BIBLE

His name is John.

SARAH RICE

10 Publishing
a division of 10 of those.com

To My Sons

Luke Stevens Rice
John Wicks Rice
Nathan Kenyon Rice
Cameron James Rice

May you love his story and reflect his glory!

First published in Great Britain in 2021

British Library Cataloguing in Publication Data
A record for this book is available from the British Library

ISBN: 978-1-913896-56-0

Designed by Pete Barnsley (CreativeHoot.com)

Printed and bound in Great Britain by Clays Ltd, Elcograf S.p.A.

10Publishing, a division of 10ofthose.com
Unit C, Tomlinson Road, Leyland, PR25 2DY, England

Email: info@10ofthose.com
Website: www.10ofthose.com

Contents

Foreword

Let's be honest. It requires a lot of effort, and a lot of patience, and a lot of creativity, and a lot of determination to nurture a Christ-focused atmosphere and conversation in our homes. So much is working against us. There's the television and the internet, sports and social media, homework and school projects. Then there's grocery shopping and laundry and ... well lots of things working to hinder us from purposefully spending time together as a family talking about the most important truths in the universe. But there is also something working for us: the goodness of the story the Bible tells and our desire for our children (and ourselves) to be captivated and shaped by that goodness.

That's why I love what Sarah Rice has put together in this Advent Devotional. During the season when parties and presents and programs can easily dominate our families' lives, this book provides a daily oasis of rich truths to talk about, a daily corrective to being pulled into a merely cultural Christmas. It sets before us and our children the only thing in the world worthy of lifelong pursuit: the glory of God.

When I was in college, the first assignment in my Bible Doctrines class was to write a paper on one word: glory. We weren't supposed to use any books or helps, just a concordance and the Scriptures themselves. I remember it being really hard. And I'm not sure I got close enough to the essence of glory to get a good grade. But it set me on a lifetime trajectory of seeking to not only understand but also to enjoy, pursue, be transformed by, and one day see the glory of God in the face of Jesus Christ. Glory is at the heart of the creation of the world, the Creator of the world, the problem with the world, and the future of the world. I pray that tracing God's glory through the pages of this book this Advent season will draw you and your family into the wonder of, and give you a greater longing for, the glory of God.

Nancy Guthrie

About This Advent Devotional

My absolute love for the Christmas season began when I was a little girl and continues still. The music, lights, decorations, family traditions, gifts, and (most of all) the mystery of God made flesh make this one of the most wonderful times of my year. As a child, the Christmas season felt just about perfect in every way, but as I've gotten older, I've realized that my view of the season was somewhat idealized in the naivety of childhood.

As wonderful as December is, the realities of living in a fallen world don't just go away during this special month. On the contrary, they're often highlighted. Busyness and stress creep in. The longer to-do lists are exhausting. Relationships are challenging. Grief is more raw than usual. Children still have meltdowns, and there is still … laundry! I've come to realize that my hope and joy must run deeper than the season itself, or I'll be let down every year.

The cliché "Jesus is the reason for the season" is almost as overused as it is true. I know that Jesus is the reason for the season—he is our hope in

December and every month of the year! But just because I *know* it's true doesn't mean I *live* as if it's true. In the hustle and bustle of the holidays, it's all too easy to make little room for Christ. If Jesus truly is the reason and hope for the season, then he must be central in my heart and home the whole month through. How do I make this my reality in the busiest month of the year when so many other things vie for my time and affections?

I have found that if Christ is not central in my life during the first eleven months of the year, he won't be central in the last month either. If I am not rooted in the Bible's big story from January to November, I will miss the sheer magnitude of what I read in Luke chapter two during December. The centrality of Christ in my own heart and in our family rhythms at Christmas is tied to my love for him and commitment to his Word every day of the year. It is also tied to my intentionality as I think and plan ahead for a Christ-focused Christmas season.

Tracing Glory: The Christmas Story Through the Bible is a twenty-five-day Advent Devotional I wrote for our family to use each December. It begins by looking back at the creation of the world in the book of Genesis and ends looking forward to the new creation in the book of Revelation, tracing the glory of Jesus Christ from start to finish. I wrote this devotional primarily for my boys because I want them to understand that the birth of Christ is the climax of a much larger story—a story about God's mission to redeem sinful people for his glory.

This Advent Devotional was written with children, teens, and adults in mind. My goal was to communicate big truths in ways a child could grasp. I want to help readers see how every individual story in the Bible points either forward or backward to the hero of the big, overarching story.

In each day's reading, there is a key Scripture given to look up as the basis for that day's devotional. Next is my written commentary on the key

Scripture. At the end of each day's reading, I have summarized the key Scripture and commentary with one main point and a Christ connection, showing how that particular Bible passage points to Jesus Christ. I have also provided three questions that will help you and your children process what you have read and then engage in discussion about it. Finally, at the end of this resource, I have provided a "Dictionary of Big Bible Words," where I've included a definition for some of the more difficult words and complex concepts throughout. You will notice that in each day's reading, some words are in bold type. When you come to a bold word as you read, you can flip to the back and refer to the dictionary to help you better understand or explain it to your child.

While preschoolers may not yet be able to grasp all the content given in the key Scripture and commentary, they will benefit from hearing the main point. I would suggest that parents of very young children read the first two sections on their own first and then communicate those truths to children at their particular level of understanding. I think most school-aged children and teens will benefit from listening to or reading the commentary, but families can decide what works best for their particular situation. This is a resource that very young children can grow into through the years.

In this resource, each day comes with a visual of an individual ornament from an entire ornament set that can be purchased with the devotional. If you have the ornament set, you can use the images to show you which ornament to pull out for the day. If not, these ornaments can be easily replicated using basic craft materials. Each day of the Advent season, have your children pull the ornament out of the bag that corresponds to the key Scripture and hang it up. Having a visual helps children grasp the meaning of the text and makes Advent exciting as they anticipate what ornament they will open each day.

The story you will encounter in this Advent Devotional is both epic and true and it isn't finished yet. We are living within this grand story now, awaiting the final chapter when we will see Christ face-to-face and dwell with him forever. My prayer is that, as we wait, God would use this resource to help us stand in awe of his matchless glory. As we encounter the breadth and length and height and depth of God's love for us in Christ, may we move to worship him every day in December and the whole year through.

For his glory alone,

Sarah Rice

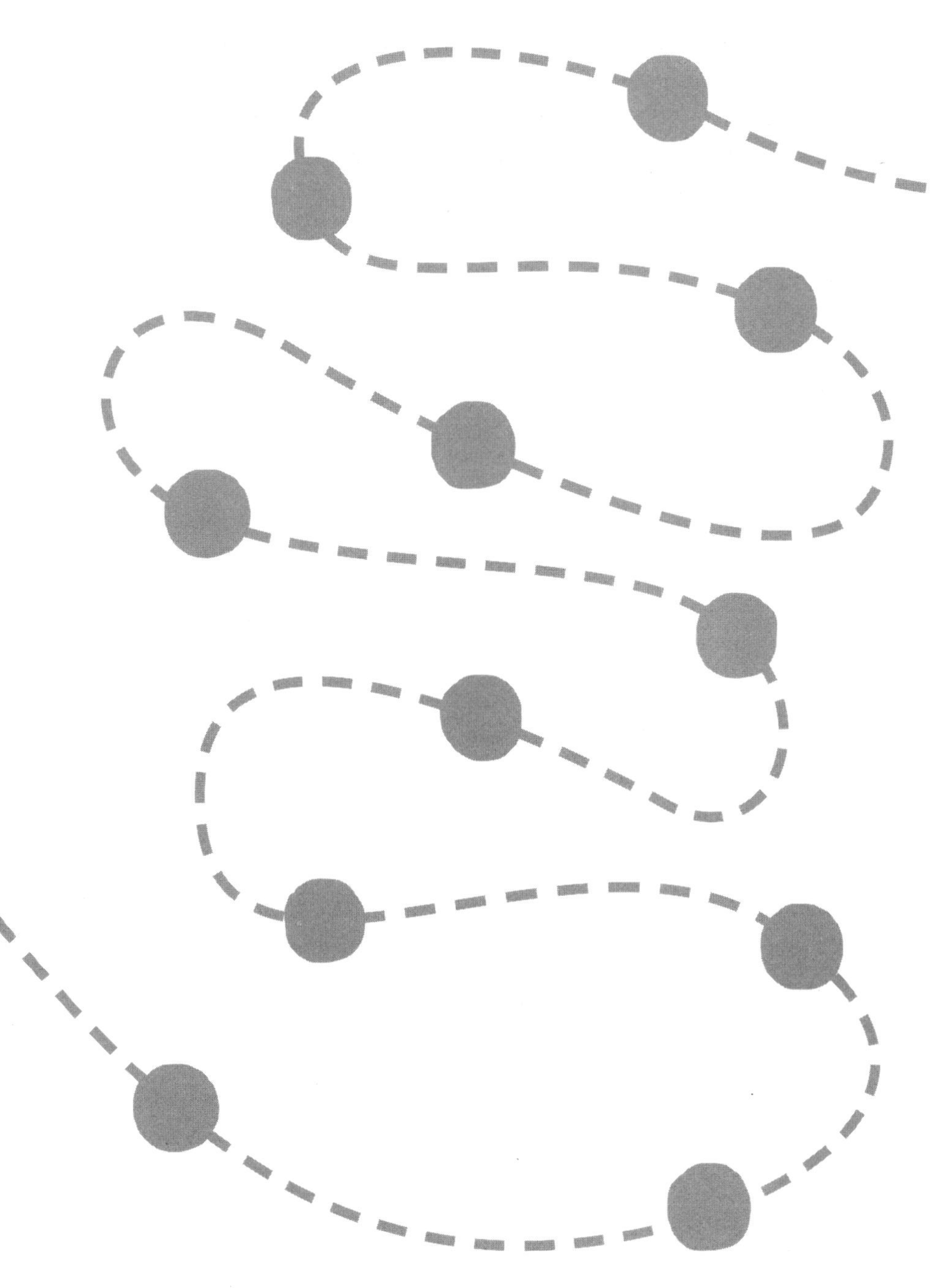

DECEMBER 1

Christmas in Creation

KEY SCRIPTURE: GENESIS 1:1–3

Did you know that the Christmas story begins on the very first page of the Bible? It begins with the words "In the beginning God..." You see, the Christmas story is one long, beautiful story about God.

Before anything else existed, God was here. No one created God. He has always been and doesn't need anything outside himself because he is enough. God doesn't need food or clothes. He doesn't get hungry like us. God doesn't get tired and need to sleep. He doesn't need love from anyone else because God himself *is* love. There are three persons in our one God—God the Father, God the Son, and God the **Holy Spirit**—and there has always been perfect love between them. In fact, there is perfect *everything* in our three-in-one God. He is **holy**—totally beautiful and good.

The first thing that the Bible tells us is that God created the heavens and the earth. God made everything. He made things we can see, like trees and animals, and he made things we can't see, like angels and faraway planets. If God doesn't need *anything*, why do you think he created *everything*?

The Bible says God created the whole world for his **glory**. This means God created everything so his perfect goodness and beauty could be enjoyed and celebrated and praised!

When God first created the earth, it was a dark blob of matter. Do you know what God made next? He made light! God made light to shine on the dark earth, so his glory could be seen by and through everything else he would create.

Later on in this story, we'll see a different kind of darkness covering the earth and keeping God's glory from being seen and enjoyed as it should be. We'll also see the true Light coming to earth to defeat that darkness and show the glory of God as it had never been seen before. The Christmas story is all about light chasing away darkness!

MAIN POINT

God has always existed. He doesn't need *anything*, but he created *everything* to bring him glory. The Christmas story begins with the creation of the world and God's light shining on it.

CHRIST CONNECTION

Jesus Christ is the true Light of the world. He brings life to **sinners** living in spiritual darkness and perfectly reveals God's glory (Jn. 1:1–5, 9; Is. 43:5–7).

DISCUSSION QUESTIONS

1. What did God create?
2. Why did God create everything?
3. Praise God for something he has made (e.g. tall mountains, a beautiful sunset, a new baby, etc.).

DECEMBER 2

Glory Reflectors

KEY SCRIPTURE: GENESIS 1:27–28

When you look in a mirror, what do you see? You see a picture of yourself! God created everything—the sun, moon, stars, mountains, oceans, trees, and animals—to be like a mirror reflecting a picture of him. We can't see God the Father with our eyes because he doesn't have a body like us. God is spirit. But when we look at God's creation, we can learn some things about him. We can see how huge and powerful and beautiful God is through what he has made. Do you know what God created to reflect the best picture of him? You and me! We are his **glory** reflectors.

God saved his very best creation for last. After making everything else, God made two human beings. He made a man named Adam and a woman named Eve. God made Adam and Eve both alike and different. They were alike because they were the only creatures on earth made in God's image. These humans were made to reflect God more clearly than anything else in all of creation and to show a true picture of him. But Adam and Eve were also made different from each other. They were made male and female. God gave them different bodies and different jobs so that, together, they could do the most important job he would give them on earth—to reflect his glory.

God put Adam and Eve in a beautiful garden in a place called Eden. He commanded them to look after the garden and care for the animals just as he would. God told Adam and Eve to have lots of children. They were to fill the earth with many more humans who would show God's glory by telling a true story about him with their lives. You are one of those children! Like Adam and Eve, you were made either a boy or girl in God's image. You were

made to reflect a picture of God so that everyone who sees you will say, "Wow! God is great!" He is the one who deserves all the praise and hoorays, because he is the one who made *you!*

All humans are created to show what God is like, but only one human born on earth has shown who God is perfectly. The Bible says when we look at this human, we see an exact picture of the invisible God! This human is the Hero of the Christmas story—the ultimate glory reflector.

MAIN POINT

God made human beings male and female in his image to show what he is like and bring him praise and glory.

CHRIST CONNECTION

Jesus Christ is a perfect picture of the God we cannot see. When he came to earth, he showed us God's glory (Col. 1:15–20).

DISCUSSION QUESTIONS

1. Who are God's "glory reflectors"?
2. Why do you think God made boys and girls different?
3. What is your favorite thing to do (e.g. play a sport or instrument, build with bricks, draw pictures, dance)? How can you show others what God is like when you do this?

DECEMBER 3

Glory Thieves

KEY SCRIPTURE: GENESIS 2:15–17; 3:1–7, 15

The garden in Eden was a wonderful place, full of beautiful trees with delicious fruit. Adam and Eve lived there and God was with them. He allowed them to eat fruit from every tree in the garden except one—the tree of the knowledge of good and evil. Adam and Eve were even allowed to eat from the tree of life and live forever. But if they disobeyed God and ate from the forbidden tree, God promised they would surely die. This tree was a test for Adam and Eve to remind them that God is the one who decides what's right and what's wrong because he is the Creator. He makes the rules because he is good, so he knows what is right and good for us.

Everything was wonderful until a snake in the garden started telling lies. The snake found Eve and began to question God's Word: *Did God really say…?* Eve started to wonder why God wouldn't let her eat the fruit from that one particular tree. Was he trying to hide something good from her? Then, the snake told a big fat lie! He told Eve she would *not* surely die if she ate from the tree of the knowledge of good and evil. The snake promised that eating the forbidden fruit would make Eve wise, just like God.

But Eve was already like God in many ways. She was made in his image to show a true picture of him. Obeying God's Word would make Eve truly wise. Sadly though, she believed being *like* God wasn't enough. Eve wanted to *be* God. She wanted to make her own rules. She didn't want to reflect God's **glory**; she wanted to steal it for herself!

Eve disobeyed God and ate the fruit. She gave some to Adam who disobeyed too, and the darkness of **sin** came into their hearts and into the

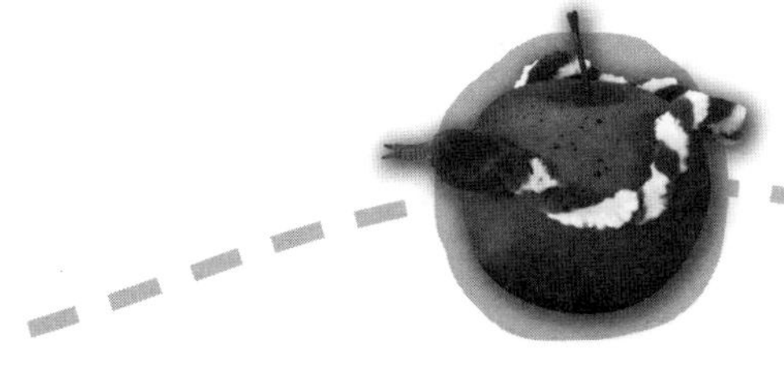

world. Sin is the choice to reject God and not trust his goodness. Humans sin when they disobey God's Word and try to steal his glory for themselves.

Because of their sin, Adam and Eve could not continue to live with God. They had to leave the garden. They could no longer see and show God's glory as they once had, and life became very hard. When Adam and Eve disobeyed God, their hearts died immediately, and one day their bodies would die, too.

This is a very sad story, isn't it? Well, it would be, if not for God. God gave Adam and Eve a promise of hope. They would still have children, and God promised that, one day, he was going to send one of those children to crush the head of that evil, lying snake. This Snake-Crusher would make everything right and good in the world again.

MAIN POINT

Adam and Eve sinned against God by disobeying his Word. Evil and pain came into the world.

CHRIST CONNECTION

Jesus Christ is the son of Adam and Eve who bruised the head of the serpent through his saving work on the cross. One day, he will crush the snake once and for all (1 Jn. 3:8; Heb. 2:14; Rev. 20:10).

DISCUSSION QUESTIONS

1. What was the one rule God gave Adam and Eve in the garden?
2. Why do you think they disobeyed God's rule?
3. What promise did God give Adam and Eve? How can that help us when we get things wrong?

DECEMBER 4

Judgment and Mercy

KEY SCRIPTURE: GENESIS 6:9–22

Sin came into the world when Adam and Eve broke God's one rule, but it grew and spread like a horrible weed, taking over the world. Adam and Eve passed sin on to their children, who passed it on to their children, and the cycle continued. Sin grew so big and bad that God decided to wipe away everything that he had created and start over with a man named Noah. God's special **grace** was on Noah. God loved him, even though Noah had a sinful heart like every other human. God had a relationship with Noah and helped him do what was right in a sinful world.

God told Noah he was going to cover the entire earth with water, wiping away everyone and everything in a flood. He commanded Noah to build a big boat called an ark. Then, God made a special promise. He promised to protect Noah, his family, and two of every kind of animal inside the ark during the flood. Noah believed God and obeyed him by building the ark. This job took many years and a lot of trust in God's Word.

After Noah finished the ark, it began to rain. For forty days and forty nights, it rained harder than you can imagine. Water fell from the sky and came up from the ground. The waters rose higher and higher, covering the tallest mountains and killing every living thing on earth.

But God rescued Noah. After Noah and his family and the animals were safe inside the ark, God shut the door. God used the ark to protect them from the violent waters outside. When the rain finally stopped and the waters dried up, God brought everyone out of the ark. Noah immediately thanked God by offering an animal **sacrifice** . A sacrifice is when sinful people kill an

innocent animal and offer it to God to make payment for sin. Noah knew that God is the one who saves, even when we don't deserve it.

The flood reminds us that sin is very bad, and God must judge sinners because he is perfectly good. God judges sinners by rightly punishing their sin. The ark reminds us that God also loves sinners. God showed **mercy** to Noah and his family in the ark by saving them from the flood even though they had sinful hearts. After the flood, God put a rainbow in the sky as a sign of his promise to never again punish sin through a worldwide flood. Many years later though, God showed his **judgment** and mercy in a different way—not through water and an ark, but through a man on a cross.

MAIN POINT

Because God is perfectly good, he must punish sin. Because God is merciful, he saves sinners who don't deserve it.

CHRIST CONNECTION

Jesus Christ is the ark! Jesus protects all sinners who hide *in him* from God's judgment against sin (Jn. 10:9; Rom. 3:23–26).

DISCUSSION QUESTIONS

1. Why did God decide to flood the world he created?
2. What is it about God's character that caused him to rescue Noah and his family?
3. When you see a rainbow in the sky, what can it remind you of? Why is this good news?

DECEMBER 5

The Tower of Pride and Glory

KEY SCRIPTURE: GENESIS 11:1–9

After the flood, God **blessed** Noah and his family. He told Noah, his three sons, and their wives to have lots of children who would spread out and fill the earth with his **glory** to make God famous. There was just one problem: Noah still had a **sinful** heart. He passed sin down to his sons, who passed it to their children, and the cycle continued.

Before long, God's people were disobeying his Word again. They decided they didn't want to spread out on the earth to make *God* famous. Instead, they wanted to stay together for their own safety and make *themselves* famous. The people settled in one area and began to build a city and a tower that would climb up to heaven. They thought they were pretty great and they wanted the whole world to know it!

But God knew his children would never be happy trying to make themselves famous without him. True happiness comes from being with God and showing his glory. And no matter how high the tower got, God's children would never be able to climb up to him on their own. So, God came down. Because he is full of **mercy** and love, God Most High leaned down low to stop the work his children were doing before they climbed any further away from him.

God made the people speak many different languages. If they could not understand each other, they could not continue to work together in one place to disobey God. Noah's big family was now forced to spread out. People who spoke the same language grouped together and then separated from groups who spoke different languages. The place of the unfinished tower was called

"Babel" (which means "mixed up") because that is where God mixed up the people's words.

The tower of Babel reminds us that we can't climb up to God, but he loves us so much that he is willing to come down to us, even while we are sinning against him. Many years after the tower at Babel, God came down to his people again. This time, he didn't come to separate them from each other *because* of sin. He came to save them *from* sin and bring them back together as one big family.

MAIN POINT

God's people disobeyed him by staying in one place and building a city and tower to make themselves famous. God came down and spread them out on earth by making them speak different languages, so that they could continue to show his glory.

CHRIST CONNECTION

Jesus Christ came down to earth to save people from their sins and bring them together as one big family (Phil. 2:5–11; Acts 2:1–8).

DISCUSSION QUESTIONS

1. How did Noah's big family disobey the command God had given them?
2. Why did they want to stay together and build a tower to heaven?
3. What is one way you try to make yourself famous rather than making God famous?

DECEMBER 6

A New Family

KEY SCRIPTURE: GENESIS 12:1–4; 15:1–6

After God mixed up people's languages at Babel, people began to spread out on the earth. Because of their **sin**, however, they were still not making God famous in the world. In fact, many people on earth did not even know God. But God didn't give up on his wonderful plan to use people to fill up creation with his **glory**.

Noah had a great, great, great, great, great, great, great, great grandson named Abram. Abram did not know the one true God, but God knew him. God chose Abram and called him to be the father of a big, new family who would be chosen to worship the one true God. This family would be God's special people who would reflect a true picture of him to the world.

God told Abram to leave his country, his people, and his old way of life. He told Abram to go to a new land that God would give him. God made a **covenant** (a very big and special promise) with Abram. He promised to **bless** Abram and his new family. God's blessing spoke about all the good things God would do for Abram. And there's more. God promised that, through Abram's family, he was going to bless people from every nation in the world! God even changed Abram's name to Abraham, which means "father of nations."

There was only one problem. Abraham and his wife Sarah could not have children. How could Abraham become the father of many nations without any children? But this was not a problem for God. God loves to take empty people and fill them up. God took Abraham outside and told him to look up and try to count the stars. God told Abraham that his children would be

like the stars in the sky—too many to count! While it seemed impossible, Abraham believed God's Word. He trusted that God would keep his promises.

Although Abraham trusted God, he was not perfect. Like all human beings, he had a sin problem. God's blessing wasn't going to come to all people on earth because Abraham was perfect or always obeyed God. He wasn't, and he didn't! No, God was going to use Abraham's big family to send someone better—someone perfect. It would be through a future child of Abraham that God would carry out his plan to save people everywhere and fill the world with his glory again.

MAIN POINT

God blessed a man named Abram (later named Abraham) and told him to leave home and start a big, new family. God would offer his blessing to the whole world through Abraham's family.

CHRIST CONNECTION

Jesus Christ is the son of Abraham through whom all the nations will be blessed. Abraham's blessing comes to us through faith in Christ (Gal. 3:14, 26–29).

DISCUSSION QUESTIONS

1. Who did God choose to be the father of a big, new family?
2. Do you think Abraham and Sarah found it easy to believe God would keep his promises to them? Why?
3. How can we know that God will keep his promises to us?

DECEMBER 7

Son and Sacrifice

KEY SCRIPTURE: GENESIS 22:1–19

Abraham obeyed God. He and Sarah left home and set out for the land God would show them. But they still didn't have a child. It started to look like God might not keep his promises after all. But God always keeps his promises. When Abraham and Sarah were very old, God gave them a son. His name was Isaac.

God promised that, through Isaac, he would continue to grow Abraham's family until they were as many as the stars and a **blessing** to people in every nation. For this plan to work, it was important for Abraham to trust God no matter what. Abraham would need to believe God was good and obey his commands even when he could not understand them.

God tested Abraham's trust and obedience. He asked Abraham to give up his only son Isaac as a **sacrifice**. A sacrifice was a way for **sinful** people to worship a perfect, **holy** God. In a sacrifice, the sinful person kills an innocent animal and gives it to God to make payment for sin. God was asking Abraham to kill his own son as the sacrifice! How could this be right?

Even when he couldn't understand God's command, Abraham trusted God and chose to obey. Abraham knew God was good and would keep his promises even if that meant he would have to bring Isaac back from the dead. Abraham took his son Isaac, and they traveled to a mountain. Isaac carried the wood for the fire to burn up the sacrifice, but he noticed they had not brought a lamb to kill. Abraham explained to his son that God would provide the sacrifice. He knew that God always provides the payment that must be made for our sin.

Abraham built an **altar**—a special table for sacrifices—and tied Isaac on top of it. As he raised the knife to obey, God said, *"Stop!"* God never meant for Abraham to kill his son, but now he knew Abraham was willing to obey him no matter what. He was willing to give God his only son—the son he loved. When Abraham looked up, he saw a ram caught by its horns in the bushes. God had provided the animal for the sacrifice. Many years later, God provided another sacrifice for sin. This time, he didn't provide a ram; he gave his only Son—the Son he loved. This perfect sacrifice paid for the sins of his people forever.

MAIN POINT

God tested Abraham's faith by asking him to give up his only son Isaac as a sacrifice. Abraham believed God's promises and chose to obey. God provided an animal to sacrifice instead.

CHRIST CONNECTION

God gave up his only Son Jesus Christ as the last and perfect sacrifice for sin (Jn. 3:16; Heb. 10:11–14).

DISCUSSION QUESTIONS

1. Who did God ask Abraham to give up as a sacrifice?
2. Why do you think Abraham chose to obey God?
3. How does this story remind us that we can trust God enough to obey him, even when it's hard? (Hint: Think about how this story points to God's sacrifice of his one and only Son on the cross for us.)

DECEMBER 8

Ladder to Glory

KEY SCRIPTURE: GENESIS 27:41–44; 28:10–17

When Isaac grew up, he married a woman named Rebekah, and they had twin boys. The older twin was named Esau, and the younger twin was named Jacob. God chose to use Jacob to continue his plan to grow Abraham's big family and fill the earth with his **glory**. But Jacob had a **sinful** heart like everyone else. He played a mean trick on his father Isaac and his brother Esau. This made Esau so angry that he wanted to kill Jacob. To stay safe, Jacob had to leave home and run away from Esau.

Jacob set out on a journey to his uncle's house, but the sun went down before he arrived. So, Jacob found a place outside to rest for the night. Using a stone as a pillow, Jacob went to sleep and had a dream. In the dream, he saw a ladder that climbed from the earth to heaven. There were angels going up and down the ladder, and God was at the top.

God spoke to Jacob through the dream, saying that he was the God of his father Isaac and grandfather Abraham. God made promises to Jacob just as he had to his father and grandfather. God promised to be with Jacob. He would keep him safe and bring him back to this land where he now slept. God promised that Jacob's family would grow very big and spread across the earth so people from every nation could be **blessed**.

Through the dream, God was showing Jacob that he would make a way for sinful people to be with God again. Remember how the people tried to make their own ladder to heaven by building a tower at Babel? Well, God showed Jacob that *he* was the one who would make a way for his people to be with him again. God would provide the ladder!

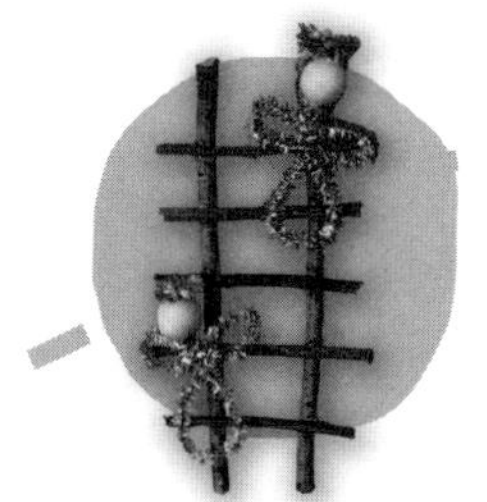

God kept his promise. He kept Jacob safe and eventually gave him twelve sons. Those twelve sons and all their many children became the nation of **Israel**—God's chosen people! It was through the nation of Israel that God provided the true ladder to heaven. But this ladder didn't look like the one Jacob saw in his dream. It looked like a person.

MAIN POINT

God blessed Isaac's son Jacob. In a dream, God showed Jacob that he would provide a ladder as the way for sinful people to get to God in heaven.

CHRIST CONNECTION

Jesus Christ is the ladder to heaven! Trusting in him to save us is the only way to get to God (Jn. 1:51).

DISCUSSION QUESTIONS

1. Abraham's son Isaac had twins named Esau and Jacob. Which twin was God going to use to keep the promises he'd made to Abraham?
2. Why do you think God's choice of Jacob was surprising?
3. Through a dream, Jacob saw that God would provide a "ladder" as a way for sinners to get to him in heaven. This ladder is Jesus! How can we trust Jesus as our true ladder to heaven?

DECEMBER 9

Evil for Good

KEY SCRIPTURE: GENESIS 45:4–8; 50:18–20

Jacob had twelve sons, but his favorite son was named Joseph. Jacob gave Joseph a special robe of many different colors. This made Joseph's brothers very jealous and angry. They hated Joseph even more when he told them about his dreams. Joseph dreamed that his brothers would one day bow down to him! The brothers were so full of hatred toward Joseph that they planned to kill him but sold him for silver to a group of travelers instead. Joseph was carried far away from his homeland to the country of Egypt as a slave.

But God had not left Joseph. He was planning to use Joseph in a big way to keep his promises to Abraham, Isaac, and Jacob. God showed Joseph the meanings of people's dreams. Joseph was able to explain the meaning of a dream for Pharaoh, the king of Egypt! He told Pharaoh there would be a terrible **famine** in the land for seven years. There wouldn't be enough food for everyone to live. In the years before the famine Pharaoh would need to save up a lot of grain to provide bread for the people during the famine. Pharaoh put Joseph in charge of this very important job of saving up grain and made him a powerful ruler in Egypt.

Joseph saved up so much grain in Egypt that people from other nations came to buy bread during the famine, including Joseph's brothers. When they arrived in Egypt, Joseph's brothers didn't recognize him. When Joseph eventually showed them who he was, his brothers were upset and afraid. They thought he might treat them badly, like they had treated him. But Joseph told them not to be afraid. He knew that the bad things his brothers had done were all part of God's good plan. God had sent Joseph to Egypt and made him powerful, so that he could provide bread for his family during the

famine. God was taking care of his chosen people! When Jacob heard that his son Joseph was alive, he and all his family moved to Egypt where they had plenty of food to eat.

Many years later, there was another son in Jacob's family who was hated by his brothers. Those brothers did terrible things to this son as well. They sold him for silver and even had him violently killed. But, once again, God used their evil actions to carry out his good plan. He used these evil actions to give us the Bread of Life—the only bread able to save the world.

MAIN POINT

Joseph's brothers treated him badly, but God used their evil actions for good. God sent Joseph to Egypt to save his family by providing them bread during the famine.

CHRIST CONNECTION

Like Joseph, Jesus Christ is the son from Jacob's family who was hated and killed by his **Jewish** brothers, but God used these evil actions to provide salvation to people from every nation. Jesus Christ is the Bread of Life, who gives our souls the nourishment we need forever (Jn. 6:32–35; Acts 2:22–24).

DISCUSSION QUESTIONS

1. How many sons did Jacob have, and which son was his favorite?
2. Give two reasons why Joseph's brothers hated him.
3. For those he loves, God always brings something good out of the bad things we face, even when it looks different than we might expect. Can you think of a time when God has brought something good out of something bad?

DECEMBER 10

Bought by Blood

KEY SCRIPTURE: EXODUS 11:4–7; 12:3–7, 12–13

Jacob's family, also called the **Israelites**, grew very big while living in Egypt. Pharaoh was afraid they would take over completely, so he made them slaves. The Egyptians forced the Israelites to work very hard and treated them badly for many years. But God had not forgotten his promises to Abraham, Isaac, and Jacob. God called an Israelite named Moses to lead his people out of slavery in Egypt. Moses told Pharaoh to let God's people go, and Pharaoh said, "No!"

So, God sent **plagues** (which are *really* terrible things that harm many people) to show Pharaoh he meant business. First, God turned the river into blood. Then, he sent frogs and bugs and hail and darkness all over the land. He made animals die and people break out with sores. God was showing that he was more powerful than all the **idols**, the fake Egyptian gods. Still, Pharaoh would not obey and let God's people go.

So, God sent one more plague—the worst one of all. The angel of death would come, and the firstborn son of every family living in Egypt was going to die. **Sin** would bring death to every family, but God would show **mercy** to his people. He told each Israelite family to kill a perfect lamb and cover its blood over the doorposts of their home. When the angel of death saw the blood on the door of a house, he would pass over it. The firstborn sons in houses covered by blood would not die because the lambs had died for them.

On the night of this last plague, there was great sadness in Egypt. Many sons died, including Pharaoh's own son. Pharaoh finally gave in and let the Israelites leave Egypt. But it wasn't long before he changed his mind and came charging after them with his army. The Israelites were camping by the

Red Sea when they saw Pharaoh coming, and there was nowhere to run. Just when things seemed hopeless, God split the sea in half and made dry land appear, so that his people could get across safely. Then, he made the waters come crashing back down on the Egyptian army.

God saved his people from death by the blood of lambs and set them free from slavery in Egypt. Sadly though, God's people were still slaves to the sin that controlled them. But one day, many years later, God would send a better Passover Lamb—his own firstborn Son—to set them free forever by his blood.

MAIN POINT

Every firstborn son in Egypt was going to die because of sin. God told the Israelite families to each kill a lamb and put its blood on the doors of their homes. The firstborn sons living in the houses covered by blood didn't die because the lambs died for them.

CHRIST CONNECTION

Jesus Christ is our Passover Lamb! Because he died for us, we can live. We are set free from sin and death by trusting in him (Jn. 1:29; 1 Cor. 5:7–8).

DISCUSSION QUESTIONS

1. What was the last and worst plague that God sent upon Egypt?
2. What did God tell the Israelites to do so that they could be rescued from this last plague?
3. The firstborn sons in houses covered by blood lived because the lambs died in their place. Who died in our place, so that we can live if we trust in him?

DECEMBER 11

The Glory of the Law

KEY SCRIPTURE: EXODUS 24:12, 15–18; 31:18

God used Moses to lead the **Israelites** out of slavery in Egypt, across the Red Sea, and into the wilderness. God had set his people free, so they could have a relationship with him. He was planning to live with them and lead them to the land he had promised to give their father Abraham. God was going to **bless** the Israelites, so they could show his **glory** to all people on earth. But for **sinful** people to live with a **holy** God, there had to be rules. Because God had set them free, the Israelites needed to know what God was like and how he expected them to live in relationship with him.

God called Moses to meet him at the top of a mountain called Sinai. God's awesome glory was displayed at Mount Sinai. The people at the base of the mountain saw thunder and lightning, fire and smoke. This reminded them that God is powerful and perfect. He cannot live where sin lives. His people must be holy like he is holy.

Moses met God at the top of the mountain. God gave him the **Ten Commandments** and the **law**, written on tablets of stone with his own finger! The law was God's rules to show the people God's perfect character. It reminded the people that they didn't have to work to earn God's love. He already loved them! *Because* God had loved them first and set them free, the law told the people to love God and worship him only. It told them to love other people in the same way they loved themselves. God promised to live with his people and bless them if they obeyed his law, and the people eagerly promised to obey.

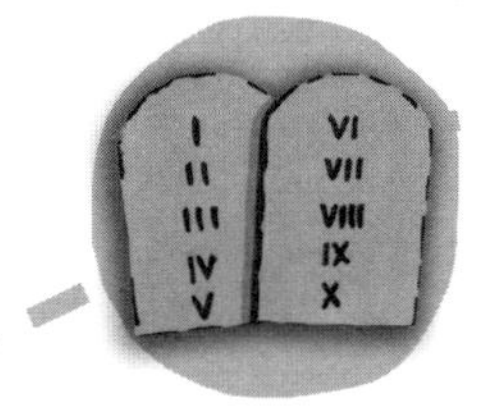

Sadly though, God's people did not keep their promise. Before Moses even came down from Mount Sinai, they had disobeyed God by creating a golden calf to worship instead of God. You see, the law showed the people how they were supposed to live, but it didn't have the power to help them obey it. God's people needed more than the law. They needed a Rescuer to keep the law perfectly in their place and give them the power they needed to obey.

MAIN POINT

God gave his people the law, written on tablets of stone. The law showed them how sinners are to live in relationship with a holy God. Because of their sinful hearts, God's people could not keep his law. It showed them their need for a Rescuer.

CHRIST CONNECTION

Jesus Christ is the Rescuer who kept God's law perfectly in the place of God's people (Gal. 3:21–26; Mt. 5:17–18).

DISCUSSION QUESTIONS

1. After God set his people free, he gave them rules to show them how to live with him and with others. What were these rules called?
2. Why are these rules good?
3. Do you sometimes find it hard to obey rules? Why?

DECEMBER 12

Shepherd King

KEY SCRIPTURE: 2 SAMUEL 7:1–13

After forty years in the wilderness, God brought the **Israelites** into the land he had promised them. Now that they were in the land God had promised, God's people wanted a human king like the nations around them. They did not want God as their true King because they wanted a king they could *see* to go out and fight their battles with them. God warned his people that a human king would take many things from them, but they kept on asking and asking. So, God gave them what they wanted.

A man named Saul was chosen as Israel's first king. Saul was the kind of king the people wanted. He looked like a king should look, but he didn't obey some very important rules God gave him. When he was confronted about his disobeying God, Saul made excuses for his sin. He did not admit, confess, and seek forgiveness from God. In doing this, Saul did not honor God as the King of kings, so the throne was taken from him, and he was no longer God's chosen king. God then chose a young shepherd boy named David to be Israel's second king. David was called a man after God's own heart. This doesn't mean David didn't have a **sin** problem. It just means David loved God and trusted him with all his heart. David sinned in some big, terrible ways, but he confessed and admitted his sin humbly to God and was forgiven.

When David became king of Israel, God was living among his people in a tent called the **tabernacle**. The tabernacle is where the tablets of stone given to Moses were kept. God's **glory** lived in the tabernacle with his people. Men called **priests** worked there, and they helped the people worship God by offering the blood of animals as **sacrifices** for the people's sins.

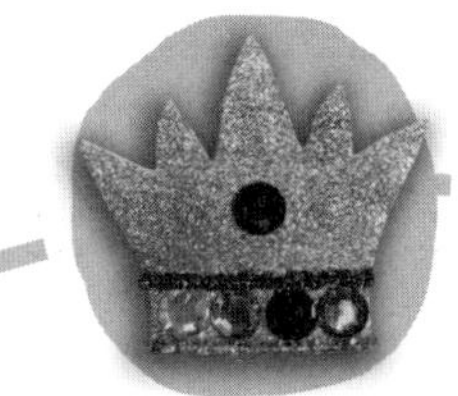

David wanted God's glory to live in a real building, not a tent. He wanted to build a permanent house for God called the **temple**. But the timing wasn't yet right. Instead, God promised to make *David* a house (which means a big family of kings) and a kingdom that would last forever! God promised that a king from David's big family would always sit on Israel's throne.

God kept his promise. Many years later, a child from David's family was born a king—the King of kings, in fact. Like David, he was also a shepherd. He called himself "the good shepherd" because, unlike any of the other kings from David's family, he had no sin and was perfectly good. This Shepherd King gave up his life to save the sheep—God's people. He was the only one able to save humans from sin *and* rule on David's throne forever.

MAIN POINT

David was a shepherd boy chosen by God to be king over his people. David's heart was fully devoted to the one true God, and God promised David a kingdom that would last forever.

CHRIST CONNECTION

Jesus is the sinless son of David. He is the Shepherd King who laid down his life for the sheep and will one day reign over the new heavens and earth forever (Lk. 1:31–33; Jn. 10:11).

DISCUSSION QUESTIONS

1. Who were Israel's first two human kings?
2. Where did God's glory live? Where did David want God's glory to live?
3. What was God's big promise to David and how does it help us today?

DECEMBER 13

A House for Glory

KEY SCRIPTURE: 1 KINGS 6:11–14; 8:10–13

God chose David's son Solomon to build the **temple**, a house where God would live with his people. Before David died, he reminded the future king, Solomon, to stay close to God and always obey his Word. For God's **glory** to live with **Israel**, it was very important for Israel's human king to love and obey the one true King.

Solomon built God's temple in the city of Jerusalem. It took seven years to finish, but it was absolutely beautiful! The walls inside were made of wood from cedar trees. Images of flowers and fruit were carved into the wooden walls, to remind the people of the beautiful garden where God had once lived with the first humans he created.

When the temple was finished, the **ark of the covenant** (a beautiful wooden chest covered in gold that held the **Ten Commandments**) was brought inside. God's glory filled the temple in a thick cloud. God was coming to live with his people again! Solomon prayed, thanking God for keeping his promises. He asked God to live with the Israelites in the temple forever and help them obey his commands. He wanted the whole world to know God and be **blessed** like Israel.

Things started well, but ended badly. Solomon disobeyed God by worshiping fake gods called **idols**, and many of his sons did the same when they ruled as king. The nation of Israel eventually split into two separate kingdoms—Israel in the north and **Judah** in the south. God judged his people for their disobedience and idol worship by sending foreign nations to invade their land and carry them away as slaves. God's glory left the temple, and it was utterly destroyed by the nation of Babylon.

But God had not forgotten his promises to Abraham and David. Years later, he brought some of his people out of slavery and back to their land again. The temple in Jerusalem was eventually rebuilt, though it was never the same. God's glory never again returned to the temple in a cloud, but many years later it returned in a baby. This baby was set apart for God at the temple in Jerusalem. He learned and taught God's Word there. He helped God's people see that *he* is the true Temple of God—the place where all of God's glory lives and will live within his people forever through the **Holy Spirit**.

MAIN POINT

King Solomon built the temple as a house for God's glory, but the Israelites worshiped idols. God punished his people for their sin, and they were carried away as slaves to other nations. God's glory left the temple, and it was destroyed.

CHRIST CONNECTION

Jesus is the true temple of God, the place where God's glory lives (Lk. 2:22–32; Jn. 1:14; Jn. 2:18–22; Col. 1:19).

DISCUSSION QUESTIONS

1. Who built the temple in Jerusalem? Describe how long it took and what it looked like.
2. God's glory came to live in the temple, but many years later, it left. Why did it leave?
3. Where does God's glory live now, and why is this very good news?

DECEMBER 14

Roots and a Shoot

KEY SCRIPTURE: ISAIAH 11:1–2, 6–10

God's people continued to disobey him by worshiping **idols**. During this time, God spoke to his people through men called **prophets**. God gave the prophet a message, and the prophet gave that message to the people. Many of the prophets warned **Israel** about the right punishment or **judgment** that God would bring if they did not stop worshiping idols. The prophets urged God's **sinful** people to come back to him before it was too late.

A man named Isaiah was one of God's prophets. He warned that God was going to use wicked, foreign nations to punish his people for continuing to disobey him. Israel and **Judah** would be attacked by their enemies. Some of God's people would be carried away from their land to be slaves in foreign nations, and others would die. Isaiah said that the nation of Israel was like God's beautiful vineyard—a field of grapevines that was going to be trampled and destroyed because of her sin (Is. 5:5-6).

The prophets spoke messages that were sad and hard to hear. They reminded the people that God must punish sin because he is **holy** and perfectly good. But the prophets also spoke messages of hope, reminding God's people that, because of his faithfulness and **mercy**, God would keep the promises he made to their fathers.

God wasn't going to let the wicked nations get away with their sin either. God's punishment for these evil nations would be like an axe, cutting down a forest of trees. Most of the forest would be destroyed, and very few trees would remain. Yet, in the midst of these promises of punishment, God gave Isaiah a message of great hope: The stump of one family tree in Judah would sprout a shoot of new life and grow again.

King David's father was Jesse. God promised that a branch of new life was going to shoot up from "the stump of Jesse" (Is. 11:1) and one day bear fruit! Isaiah wasn't talking about an actual stump and branch. He was using these things as word-pictures to help God's people understand that God would keep the promise he made to David. A King from the roots of David's family tree would sit on the throne forever!

The final King to sit on David's throne would have God's Spirit on him. He would love and obey God perfectly. One day, he would rule over the earth and bring total peace, making all things right and good again. People from every nation in the world would finally see God's **glory** and be brought together to live with him, safe from all their enemies.

MAIN POINT

God used foreign nations to punish his disobedient people, but he promised that a perfect King from David's family was coming to make all things right and sit on the throne forever.

CHRIST CONNECTION

Jesus is the true King who came from Jesse and David's family (Ac. 13:22–23).

DISCUSSION QUESTIONS

1. What word-picture did the prophet use to help God's people understand that God would keep his promise?
2. How do you think God's people felt when they heard about God's punishment for their sin?
3. The prophet Isaiah tells us that our world won't be messed-up forever. Why? How does this give you hope?

DECEMBER 15

The Suffering Lamb

KEY SCRIPTURE: ISAIAH 53:2–6, 10–11

Yesterday, we learned about how God told Isaiah that a young plant would shoot up from the stump of David's family tree. This meant that a new baby would one day be born into Abraham and David's big family. This baby would grow up to be the promised Shepherd King who would rule forever on David's throne and make the world right and good again.

God told Isaiah the Shepherd King would not be anything special to look at on the outside He would not be rich and powerful like most kings. He would not be handsome and strong like David. Many of God's people would actually hate and reject him. They would not recognize who he was or understand the work he had come to do.

Before the Shepherd King would sit on David's throne, he would go to war against the lying snake from the garden. This battle would hurt him terribly. The Shepherd King would do nothing wrong, but he would be beaten and killed. Why? Well, **sin** had caused God's people to run far away from him, like lost sheep wandering away from their shepherd. If a **holy** God was going to live with his children on earth, the price for sin had to be paid once and for all. And it had to be paid with blood.

For years, God had provided lambs for his people to **sacrifice** as a way to make payment for their sin. The lambs were killed and their blood was offered to God by the **priests** in the **temple**. The lambs died, so the people could live. But new lambs had to be killed again and again, day after day because the blood of animals was never enough to pay for human sin. God's people needed a sinless human to become the lamb that was sacrificed to pay for their sin.

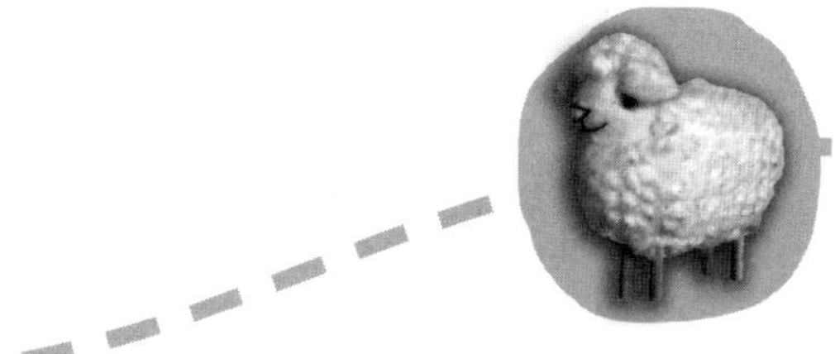

God was telling Isaiah that the promised Shepherd King from David's family would willingly become the Lamb for God's people! Without fighting back, the Lamb of God would suffer, bleed, and die a terrible death to pay for sin once and for all. The Lamb would die, so God's people could live and be seen as perfect by God.

MAIN POINT

The Shepherd King would have no sin; therefore, he would be the perfect sacrificial Lamb for sinners. He would suffer and die to pay the price for human sin.

CHRIST CONNECTION

Jesus Christ is the Lamb of God who suffered for sinners *and* the Shepherd King who reigns forevermore on David's throne (1 Pet. 2:22–25).

DISCUSSION QUESTIONS

1. Name some ways the Shepherd King was going to be different than what people might expect a king to be.
2. Why do we no longer have to kill lambs and offer their blood to God to pay for our sin?
3. Give thanks to God for sending the Shepherd King to willingly die for us.

DECEMBER 16

New Hearts, New Hope

KEY SCRIPTURE: JEREMIAH 17:9; 31:31–33; EZEKIEL 36:26–28

Like Isaiah, other **prophets** warned God's people that he would punish their idol worship through terrible attacks from foreign nations if they did not repent. Everything happened exactly as God said it would. The nations of Assyria and Babylon attacked the land. Many of God's people were carried away to be slaves in these foreign lands.

Things seemed hopeless. The **temple** where God had once lived with his people was burned down, and the city of Jerusalem was in ruins. No king from David's family was ruling on the throne. Many of God's people were far from home, separated from each other and their land. Years before, God had given his people the **law** written on tablets of stone. Although they'd promised to obey it, they failed miserably by rejecting his Word and worshiping **idols**. While God gave them many chances to return to him and obey, they could never do it because they didn't want God. Prophets named Jeremiah and Ezekiel said their hearts were sick with **sin**.

But God is faithful to keep his promises even when his people fail. Through the prophets, God made promises to bring a group of his people out of slavery and back to their land. Then, God made a new promise to **Israel** and **Judah**. He promised to give them brand new hearts!

God was going to take out their cold, dead, sin-sick hearts and replace them with new hearts full of spiritual life. The law that had been written on tablets of stone would now be written on these new hearts. God was also going to send his **Holy Spirit** to live inside his people. With new hearts and God's Spirit inside them, the people would finally *want* to obey God!

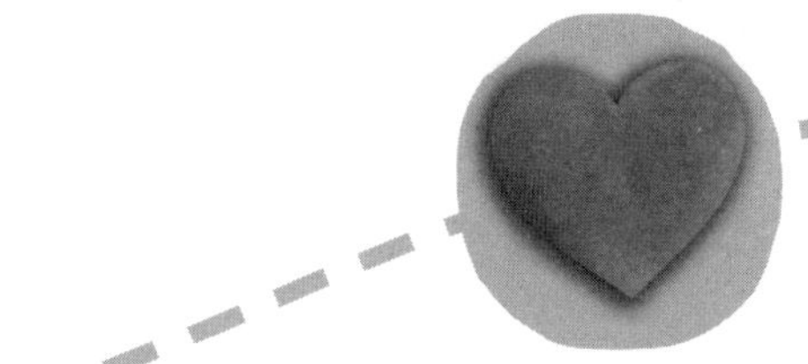

And there's more! God promised to forgive the sins of his children once and for all. How could a **holy** God, who must punish evil, forgive all those sins forever and ever? He could do it through the death of the perfect Lamb—the Lamb who obeyed God perfectly and whose blood would pay the full price for sin.

MAIN POINT

God promised to give his children new hearts, so they could obey his Word and bring him **glory**. He promised to forgive their sins, so they could live with him forever.

CHRIST CONNECTION

Jesus Christ died once to pay the full price for human sin. Because his blood was shed, God forgives his children and gives them new hearts (Heb. 10:11–18; Mt. 26:27–28).

DISCUSSION QUESTIONS

1. Why did God's people keep disobeying his Word over and over again?
2. How do you think God's people felt when they were slaves in a foreign land? What promise of hope did God give them during this time?
3. All people who are trusting in God's perfect Lamb to forgive their sins have been given a helper to live inside them and help them want to obey God's law. Who is this helper?

DECEMBER 17

His Name is John

KEY SCRIPTURE: LUKE 1:13–17, 67–79

God spoke to his people through **prophets** for many years. The last prophets spoke to God's people when they returned from slavery to their own land and rebuilt the **temple** and the city of Jerusalem. Although they had been allowed to return, **Israel** and **Judah** were still under the control of foreign nations. No king from David's family was on the throne. In fact, there was no sign of the promised Shepherd King, and then God went silent. He didn't speak to his people through a prophet for four hundred years! Was God going to keep his promises to Abraham and David?

One ordinary day, the long silence was broken by an angel named Gabriel. Gabriel appeared to a **priest** named Zechariah as he was working in the temple. The angel told Zechariah that he and his wife Elizabeth (who were both old and had no children) would have a son named John. John would have God's Spirit in him before he was even born. He would grow up to be a great prophet of God, who would tell people an important message of good news. John would tell God's people to turn away from their **sin** because the kingdom of God was coming on earth. John would prepare the way for the Shepherd King!

Zechariah could not believe what this angel was telling him. He asked for a sign, so he could know this was true. Because Zechariah doubted God's Word with his mouth, the angel closed his mouth. This was his sign: Zechariah would not be able to speak until the birth of his son. When the baby was born, some relatives and neighbors thought he should be named after his father. Zechariah wrote on a tablet, "His name is John," and immediately his

mouth was opened. Full of joy, Zechariah praised God for being a God who remembers his people. God's promises were coming true after all!

John grew up to live an unusual life. He stayed in the wilderness, wearing clothes made of camel's hair and eating locusts and honey. But John was the greatest prophet to ever live because he saw the King that God's people had been waiting for, and he pointed people to him. John understood that this King was also the final Passover Lamb—the one who would die, so God's people could live. When John saw the Shepherd King coming toward him, he said, "Look! There he is… the Lamb of God, who takes away the sin of the world!"

MAIN POINT

After four hundred years of silence, God sent John the Baptist as a prophet to get God's people ready for the Messiah—the Shepherd King from David's family who would save God's people.

CHRIST CONNECTION

John prepared the way for Jesus Christ, the son of David and Son of God (Jn. 1:29; Mt. 11:7–11).

DISCUSSION QUESTIONS

1. Who did Gabriel appear to, and what news did he bring?
2. Why was John the greatest prophet who ever lived?
3. Discuss one way you and your family can point someone to the "Lamb of God, who takes away the sins of the world" during this season.

DECEMBER 18

Mother by Miracle

KEY SCRIPTURE: LUKE 1:26–38

Not long after the Angel Gabriel visited Zechariah in the **temple**, he made another important visit. This time, he came to a young **Jewish** girl named Mary (Jew was the name for God's people who lived in the southern kingdom of **Judah**). Mary lived in the small town of Nazareth and was engaged to Joseph, a man from King David's family. Mary was not royal, rich, or famous. She was simple, ordinary, and young. But Mary knew the promises God had made to her people. She believed God's Word and was waiting for the coming Savior and King.

When Gabriel appeared to Mary, she was surprised and scared but he told her not to be afraid because she was "highly favored." God loved Mary, and his special **grace** was on her. Gabriel told Mary she was going to have a baby boy who would be named Jesus. He went on to tell her that this baby was the promised Shepherd King from David's family who would one day rule on David's throne and reign forever!

Mary was confused. How could she have a baby? She and Joseph were not yet married, and she had never been with any man in a way that would make a baby possible. Gabriel explained that this baby would not come into existence through a human man; God would fill up Mary's empty womb through the power of the **Holy Spirit**. Mary's pregnancy would be a **miracle**, an amazing work of God, and baby Jesus would be the Son of God! He would be perfectly good and **holy**—not born with a **sinful** heart like all other human beings. It sounded absolutely impossible, but Mary knew nothing was impossible for her powerful God. She believed God's Word to her from Gabriel, and she was happy to do what God wanted – to be a part of his plan.

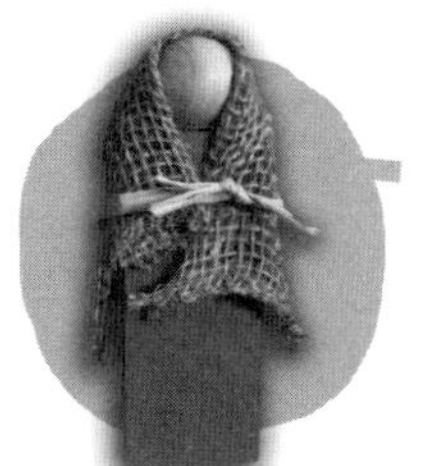

Not long after the angel's announcement, Mary visited her cousin Elizabeth (who was pregnant with Jesus' cousin John). When Mary arrived, baby John kicked joyfully inside Elizabeth. Even before he was born, John recognized the Shepherd King. Mary's heart was so full of joy that she burst out in a song of praise to God, thanking him for providing a Savior for those in need of saving. Mary praised God for using simple, ordinary people like her as part of his big plan. She gave God **glory** for remembering the promises he had made to Abraham so many years ago. Mary understood that, through this son of Abraham growing in her womb, God was going to **bless** people from every nation on earth.

MAIN POINT

The angel told Mary she was going to have a baby named Jesus. This baby would be from the Holy Spirit. He would be the Son of God and the King from David's family who would save God's people and rule forever.

CHRIST CONNECTION

Mary understood that Jesus was the promised Shepherd King and the fulfillment of God's promises to Abraham. Mary's miracle pregnancy was a sign that God was going to keep his promises (Lk. 1:46–47, 54–55; Is. 7:14).

DISCUSSION QUESTIONS

1. What news did the Angel Gabriel give to Mary and how did she respond?
2. Explain why the baby growing inside Mary was a miracle.
3. Do you ever feel like you're too young or ordinary to be used by God? How does today's reading remind you that this is not true?

DECEMBER 19

Father by Faith

KEY SCRIPTURE: MATTHEW 1:18–25

At the time the Angel Gabriel told Mary she would have a baby, she was about to be married to a man called Joseph. The Bible says Joseph was a **righteous** man. This means he worshiped the one true God and did his very best to faithfully obey God's **law** and give him **glory**. Like Mary, Joseph believed God would keep the promises he had made to Abraham, Isaac, Jacob, and David. Joseph was from King David's big family, and he knew the Shepherd King would come from his family tree. Could he have imagined that this Promised King would be his own son?

When Joseph found out Mary was going to have a baby, he was surprised and sad. Joseph knew this baby had not come from him. He assumed Mary had broken her marriage promise to him, and the baby had come from another man. Joseph decided he would not take Mary as his wife. He planned to end their relationship quietly because he loved Mary and did not want her to experience shame and punishment from breaking God's **law** about marriage.

But one night, as Joseph slept, an angel from God appeared to him in a dream. The angel told Joseph not to be afraid to take Mary as his wife because the baby inside her was not from another man. Mary's baby was from the **Holy Spirit** of God! The angel told Joseph the baby's name would be Jesus (which means "God saves") because he would save God's people from their **sins**. This was the baby they had been waiting for—the promised Shepherd King who would rescue God's people.

Joseph believed the Word of God through the angel and he obeyed. He took Mary as his wife and, after Jesus was born, Joseph adopted him as his

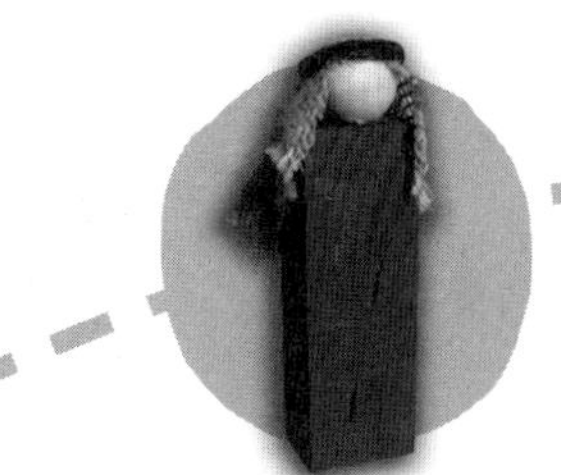

own son. It would not have been easy for Joseph. Many people would not believe that this baby had come from the Holy Spirit. But Joseph cared more about obeying God than he cared about what other people thought. He believed God's Word even when he could not see what the future would hold. God used Joseph's faith and obedience to bring King Jesus into the big family of David as a forever son.

MAIN POINT

An angel appeared to Joseph in a dream. The angel told him not to be afraid to take Mary as his wife because the baby inside her was from the Holy Spirit. Joseph believed God's Word to him and obeyed. He became Jesus' earthly father.

CHRIST CONNECTION

Jesus Christ is a son of David through his earthly father Joseph (Mt. 1:15–17).

DISCUSSION QUESTIONS

1. What did Joseph plan to do when he found out Mary was going to have a baby? Why?
2. What made Joseph change his mind?
3. It's not always easy to obey God. Ask God to help you live to please him most of all.

DECEMBER 20

A Picture of Glory

KEY SCRIPTURE: LUKE 2:1–7

During the time Mary and Joseph lived, God's people were under the control of the nation of Rome. The leader of Rome made a law that everyone must travel to his hometown to be counted in order to pay taxes. So, Joseph and Mary made a trip to Bethlehem, the town of Joseph's family tree. Bethlehem was known as "the city of David" because that was where King David was born and chosen as king.

After Mary and Joseph arrived in Bethlehem, it was time for Mary to have her baby. Unfortunately, the inn where travelers could stay was completely full of other visitors. Mary and Joseph found no place to stay except the place where the animals were kept. Mary gave birth to her firstborn son, the promised King and Savior from David's family, among animals. The King that God's people had been waiting and longing for was finally here! Mary wrapped the baby tightly in strips of cloth to keep him warm and laid him in the manger, the box of hay where the animals ate their food. Eight days after his birth, they called the baby Jesus, just as the angel had told them.

Wouldn't a palace have been a better place for the King of kings to be born? How strange for him to enter this world in a shelter with animals. Then again, it's not so strange when you remember that this King was also a lamb—*the* Lamb who would die for human **sinners**. This baby's birthplace was no surprise to God. God was showing the world that he was coming down, even to the lowest of places, to rescue his people and live with them again. And this time, the Creator of the universe wouldn't live with his people in a garden or a **temple**. He would live with them in a human body, a body just like theirs.

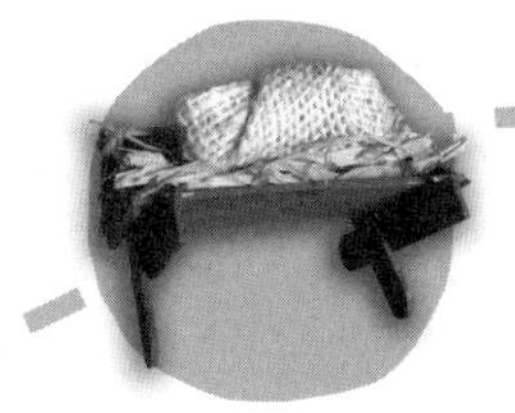

Like every other baby, Jesus got tired and hungry. He needed to sleep and eat. He felt everything other human beings feel: pain, sadness, anger, joy, and love. But, even as he grew up, Jesus had no sin. He reflected God's image perfectly, showing the world exactly what God is like. This child, both truly human and truly God, was a walking picture of God's **glory** for everyone to see.

MAIN POINT

Mary gave birth to her baby in Bethlehem and laid him in a manger. This baby, named Jesus, was both truly God and truly human. He was a living picture of God's glory.

CHRIST CONNECTION

Jesus Christ is the long-awaited Shepherd King and Lamb of God promised through all of Scripture. He is the exact image of God and shows a picture of God's glory in a way humans can see (Jn. 1:14, 18; Heb. 1:1–3).

DISCUSSION QUESTIONS

1. Where was the promised Shepherd King born?
2. Explain why Jesus' birth place was both strange and not strange at all.
3. Describe several ways Jesus was just like all other babies. Then, describe the one way He was different from all other babies. Why is this difference very good news for us?

DECEMBER 21

Birth Announcement

KEY SCRIPTURE: LUKE 2:8–18

On the night Jesus was born, a group of shepherds were watching over their sheep in a field near Bethlehem. All of a sudden, an angel appeared, and the bright light of God's **glory** lit up the dark field! The shepherds were surprised and very scared, but the angel told them not to be afraid because he was bringing good news. This news was going to fill their hearts up with happiness. And this good news was not just for the shepherds; it was for all **sinful** people in need of saving.

The angel announced that the Savior and King that everyone was waiting for had been born in the city of David! The shepherds would recognize him because he was wrapped in strips of cloth and sleeping in a manger. Suddenly, an entire army of angels lit up the sky! These angels sang praises to God in heaven, giving him glory for sending the Savior who would restore peace on earth between sinful humans and a **holy** God.

This was the best and brightest birth announcement you could ever imagine! The angels were announcing the arrival of the one who God had promised from the very beginning ... the child of Adam and Eve who would bruise the snake's head ... the one from Abraham's family who would bring **blessing** to all the families of the world ... the Shepherd King from David's family who would become the Lamb and save God's people!

This birth announcement did not come first to rich, powerful, or really good people. No, shepherds were the first ones to hear about the birth of God's Lamb. Poor, smelly, sinful shepherds were the first to hear the good news about Jesus announced loud and clear!

The shepherds were so excited that they ran to see the baby. They found him in the manger, just like the angel had said. After seeing the baby with their own eyes, the shepherds couldn't keep this good news to themselves. They told everyone, and they praised God and gave him glory for keeping his promises to his people.

MAIN POINT

An angel announced the good news of baby Jesus' birth to a group of shepherds watching over their sheep at night. Many angels lit up the sky, singing praises to God for sending the Savior of his people!

CHRIST CONNECTION

The good news of Jesus Christ was announced first to **Jewish** shepherds who couldn't keep it to themselves. Soon, this good news would be announced to all kinds of people from all nations on earth (Rom. 1:16).

DISCUSSION QUESTIONS

1. Who were the first people to hear the good news about the Shepherd King's birth?
2. Describe how the shepherds found out that Jesus had arrived. Then what did they do?
3. Who is the good news about the Shepherd King's birth for?

DECEMBER 22

Guiding Star

KEY SCRIPTURE: MATTHEW 2:1–11

Just as God announced the arrival of Jesus to the shepherds in an amazing way, he announced Jesus' arrival to another group of people in an equally amazing way. God used a bright star to tell a group of men called Magi about the birth of the long-awaited Savior and King.

The Magi lived in East Asia, far from Bethlehem. The Magi were known as wise men. They were experts in mysteries like magic and dream telling, and they studied space and the stars. When Jesus was born, God made a new star appear in the sky. The Magi saw this star and knew that a great King had come into the world.

The Magi made a long trip to the city of Jerusalem. They asked people where they could find this new King because they wanted to worship him and give him **glory**. Now, at that time, a man called Herod was ruling as a king over God's people. Herod was not from Abraham and David's big family. He did not know the one true God. When Herod heard that the Magi were looking for a new king, he became very jealous and afraid. Herod did not want this new king to take his throne, so he told the Magi to find the baby and come back to tell him where he was. Herod pretended he wanted to worship the baby king too, but he really wanted to kill him.

God made the new star move in the sky. The hearts of the Magi were filled with happiness as the star guided them to the house where Mary, Joseph, and Jesus were staying. When the Magi entered the house and saw Jesus, they bowed low to worship him. They gave him presents fit for a king—gold, frankincense, and myrrh. God warned the Magi in a dream not to tell wicked Herod that they had found Jesus, so they went home a different way.

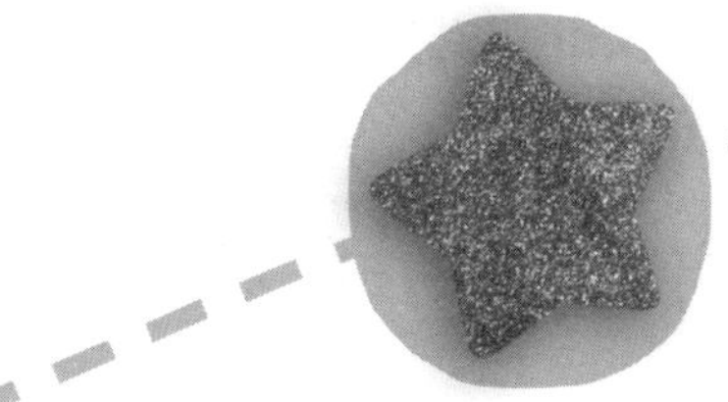

How unexpected and amazing that God led these Magi from so far away all the way to Bethlehem to bow before the one true God and King! The promises God had made to Abraham were already starting to come true. God was beginning to show people from other nations the good news about King Jesus, so he could **bless** them by forgiving their **sins** and bringing them into his big family.

MAIN POINT

The Magi were wise, powerful, and rich men from far away in the east who used a star to guide them to Jesus so they could worship him as the one, true King!

CHRIST CONNECTION

The good news of Jesus Christ is not just for the nation of **Israel** but for people from every tribe and nation on earth—even those who are far away, like us (Eph. 2:12–13, 17–19).

DISCUSSION QUESTIONS

1. Who were the Magi, and where were they from?
2. Explain how this story shows that God was keeping the promises he had made to Abraham many years before.
3. No one is too "far away" from Jesus to be rescued. Think of someone who seems far away from God. Pray and ask him to rescue that person through Jesus.

DECEMBER 23

Glory Through Death

KEY SCRIPTURE: ACTS 2:22–32

As he grew up, Jesus was a normal boy in many ways. He learned to walk, talk, and read. He slept, ate, laughed, and cried like you and me. He had parents, brothers, and sisters. But Jesus was different from other children in many ways too. From a young age, he understood God's Word in a way that amazed others. And Jesus never **sinned**—ever. He obeyed his parents and loved others perfectly. Most of all, he obeyed and loved God perfectly. His one purpose was to please God by doing what God wanted.

When he grew up, Jesus began to tell everyone the good news that God's kingdom was coming on earth. The kingdom God had promised—where the Shepherd King from David's family would rule forever—was finally coming true. Jesus called people to turn away from their sin and believe the good news that *he* was the promised King from God who would save them. He healed the sick, made the blind see, made the crippled walk, and forgave sins. Jesus was showing the world that he had the power to heal sinful hearts and everything else that sin had broken.

But God's own people, who knew God's promises to them, did not believe Jesus. They did not recognize him as the Shepherd King sent from God. In fact, the **Jewish** religious leaders hated Jesus. They were jealous because of his power and because so many people followed him. So, they decided to have him killed. Although he had done nothing wrong, Jesus was arrested like a criminal. He was whipped and beaten until he bled. He was spit on and mocked by those he had created. Then, he was nailed to a wooden cross, and he died between two criminals.

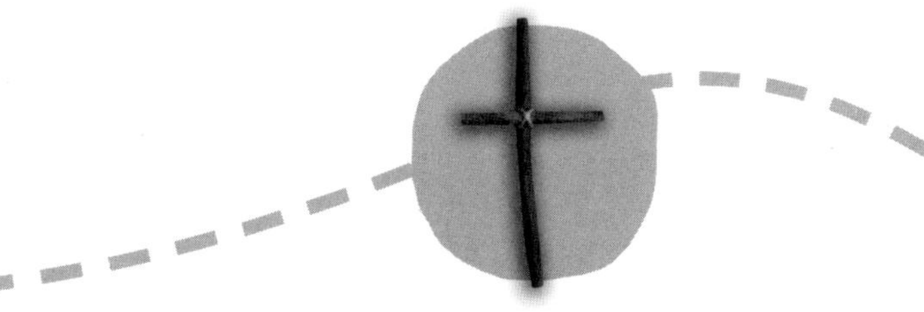

How could Jesus save God's people and rule forever as the true King if he wasn't alive? Once again, it looked as if God might not keep his promises to Abraham and David. But God was not surprised by Jesus' death. It was his perfect plan to use this evil for good. Jesus could have saved himself from death if he had wanted to, but he wanted to give **glory** to God by saving others. So, he offered himself to God as the final Lamb—the perfect human **sacrifice** for sinners. When Jesus died, he took God's full punishment for sin on himself, so God's people could be forgiven and live with him again.

Jesus didn't stay dead, though! Three days later, God raised him from death to rule forever. Jesus Christ has beaten sin and death! In him, God's says "Yes!" to keeping all of his promises.

MAIN POINT

Jesus was born to die a terrible death on a cross. He took God's punishment for sinners on himself, so sinful people could be forgiven and live with God again. After three days, God raised Jesus from the dead to rule forever.

CHRIST CONNECTION

Jesus is the "Yes!" answer to all of God's promises (2 Cor. 1:20; Heb. 9:26b–28).

DISCUSSION QUESTIONS

1. During his time on earth, what did Jesus do that showed he had power to heal sinful hearts and all sin had broken?
2. What did Jesus do so that we could be forgiven and live with him again?
3. How does today's reading remind us that, even when things look hopeless, evil will not win in the end?

DECEMBER 24

The City of Glory

KEY SCRIPTURE: REVELATION 21:1–5, 9–11

Forty days after Jesus came back to life, he went back into heaven. God's Kingdom was not going to come all at once, like people expected. It would come in stages. Before Jesus ruled as King on earth, he was going to rule as King in the hearts of those who trusted him to save them.

Before he left, Jesus gave his followers a mission. He told them to spread the good news of his saving work to people from every nation, calling others to turn away from their **sin** and trust Jesus alone for forgiveness. Jesus promised to be with his disciples. He was going to send God's own Spirit, the **Holy Spirit,** to live inside them and empower them. Jesus promised that one day he would come back to rule on earth as King.

As the disciples obeyed, the good news about Jesus began to spread to people from every tribe and nation in the world. People who believed the good news and trusted Jesus to save them became the new people of God, the church. The church is not a building but a group of people where God's Spirit lives and where Christ rules as a perfect King. The church is now God's chosen nation—the new **Israel** of God.

Although Christ rules as King over his church, things are still not as they should be in the world. The snake is still lying and convincing people God's Word isn't true. There is still pain, sadness, sickness, and death. People still sin and do not reflect God's **glory** perfectly, even those who are part of the church. But it won't be like this forever. King Jesus is coming back to earth to get rid of sin and the lying snake for good.

When he comes back, Jesus will rule as King over the earth and make everything right. He will build a new city for all the people who have trusted

him to be their Savior. This city will be perfectly safe, clean, and beautiful because God will live there. There will be no tears, pain, or death in this city. There will be no sun because God's glory will be the light. There will be no **temple** because Jesus *is* the Temple where God lives with his people. In this city, the children of God will eat from the Tree of Life, drink the Living Water, and live forever. They will shine brightly with the glory of God, and everyone will see and worship King Jesus forever!

MAIN POINT

Jesus Christ is coming back to earth to rule as King and make all things new and good. He will establish a perfect city where God will live with his people. They will reflect his glory forever.

CHRIST CONNECTION

Jesus Christ will establish the new and perfect city of God—the city Abraham and all of God's people look forward to (Heb. 11:8–10).

DISCUSSION QUESTIONS

1. Where did Jesus go forty days after he rose from the grave?
2. What mission did Jesus give his followers? How do we know they obeyed him?
3. When Jesus comes back to earth, he is going to build the "City of Glory" for all people who have trusted him to save them. What part of the future "City of Glory" excites you the most?

DECEMBER 25

Come, Let Us Adore Him

Merry Christmas! We've spent the past twenty-four days tracing God's **glory** through the pages of his beautiful story, and I pray our hearts have been stirred to respond. God has revealed himself to us through his Word so that we may experience the joy of knowing and worshiping him! This story is *our* story.

God created us in his image to live in joyful relationship with him and to spread his glory around the world. But, like Abraham, Jacob, David, and every other person in the Bible, we were born with cold, dead, **sin**-sick hearts, passed down from our first parents Adam and Eve. The Bible says we are born spiritually dead and are slaves to sin (Eph. 2:1–2). Sin has separated us from God, and, because of our sin, we don't want to come back to him or reflect his glory (Rom. 3:10–12).

Separated from God, we live in spiritual darkness, searching for something to fill the empty space in our hearts that only God can fill. Sometimes, we ignore God in the world he created and work to build our own towers for selfish glory. We believe that being really good at something, having a lot of fun stuff, or being liked by other people will fill up our empty hearts. Other times, we work hard to obey God's rules in our own power. We build towers of good behavior and try to climb up to him through our own works.

But God knows we can't get back to him on our own. No matter how hard we try, we can never be good enough. And none of the good things we do or the fun things we have can make us happy forever apart from God himself. Because of our sin, we deserve the just **judgment** of a **holy** God and to be separated from him forever.

But, the good news of Christmas is that God has not given us what we deserve. He sent a Rescuer as a human being to bring us back to him. This

Rescuer is the Ark who protects us from the flood of God's holy punishment He's the Lamb whose blood covers us and saves us from death. He's the Ladder who provides a way for us to live with God and see his glory. This Rescuer was born as a baby to live a life perfectly obeying God and die a horribly painful death for sinners, like us. This Rescuer rose from the dead and is coming back to earth as the Shepherd King who will rule forever in the light of his glory.

How do we respond to this holy God who has provided this perfect Rescuer? First, we must agree that we desperately need to be rescued. We must realize that we need to be forgiven for our sins against God. Then, we must turn away from those sins and turn to Jesus. We must trust that Jesus kept God's **law** and took God's punishment for us. We must trust what he has done so that we can be saved from sin and brought back to live with God forever. God is the only one who will fill up our empty hearts. Have you trusted Jesus to rescue you from your sins and bring you back to God? If you have not done this and would like to, you can ask God or pray the prayer below.

Then, we worship. We praise God and give him glory for all he is and all he has done through his Rescuer. We wait with hope for the day when we will together shout, "The kingdoms of this world are become the kingdoms of our Lord, and of his Christ!" (Rev. 11:15, KJV). Until then and forevermore, come, let us adore him!

PRAYER

Dear God, I know that I am a sinner. I have run away from you and have disobeyed you. Thank you for sending Jesus to rescue me from my sins. I believe Jesus lived a perfect life without sin. I believe he died on the cross and rose from the dead to save me. Please forgive me and rescue me. Help me to give God glory with my life! Amen.

DICTIONARY OF

Big Bible Words

Altar – a special table for **sacrifices.**

Ark of the covenant – A beautiful wooden chest covered in gold that held the **Ten Commandments.**

Bless/Blessing – A good thing that God promises to do for his people. Also when God gives his special **grace** or favor to people.

Covenant – A big and special promise made by God.

Famine – A time when there isn't enough food for everyone.

Glory – The power and perfect goodness and beauty of God, that should be praised and celebrated.

Grace – A gift from God that we do not deserve.

Holy – Describes God, who is completely good and perfect and has no **sin**. Also describes people who have been declared perfect by God.

Holy Spirit – God's own Spirit, who was sent to live in God's people. The Holy Spirit is God, just like God the Father and God the Son.

Idols – Fake gods that people worship instead of the one true God.

Israel/Israelites – God's chosen people who were part of Jacob's big family.

Jews/Jewish – The name for God's people who lived in the southern kingdom of **Judah** after the kingdom split.

Judah – The southern kingdom of the **Israelite** people.

Judgment – God's just and right punishment for people's **sins**.

Law – God's rules to show people God's perfect character.

Mercy – When God does not punish his people as they deserve, but shows them love instead.

Miracle – An amazing work of God.

Plagues – Terrible things that harm many people. God sent these to Pharaoh to show his **glory** and to make Pharaoh set the **Israelites** free.

Priests – Men who served God in a special way and made **sacrifices** for the people. They worked in the **tabernacle** and the **temple**.

Prophets – God's messengers, who told people God's warnings and promises.

Righteous – Describes someone who worships the one true God and faithfully obeys his **law**.

Sacrifice – Where a **sinful** person kills an innocent animal and gives it to God to make payment for **sin**. Later, Jesus would be the sacrifice to pay for all our **sin**.

Sin/Sinful – A wrong way that we live when we do not love and obey God or give him **glory**.

Tabernacle – A special tent where the tablets of stone given to Moses were kept. It was where God's **glory** lived with his people.

Temple – A beautiful house where God's **glory** lived with his people. Solomon built God's temple in the city of Jerusalem.

Ten Commandments – Ten rules written on stone that God gave his people to show them how to live his way.

A Taste of Asia
21 Devotional Adventures for the Family
BIBLE STORIES every CHILD SHOULD KNOW
The KING and the SHEPHERD BOY
Written by SAM BREWSTER Illustrated by HANNAH GREEN
Love Came Down
BETHAN LYCETT
HANNAH STOUT

10 Publishing
a division of 10 of those.com